THIS RETREAT GUIDE BELONGS TO:

_____

USED FOR / ON THE OCCASION OF:

_____

THE RULE
OF LIFE

ABOUT THE CHATTANOOGA HOUSE OF PRAYER

We are a non-profit ministry based in Chattanooga, TN.

OUR MISSION — We are seeking the transformation of our city through unified prayer, worship, and action.

—

If you are holding this guide, you have been prayed for.

TABLE OF CONTENTS

Introduction

This book serves as an essential guide for your prayer retreat. The retreat can be done individually or in a group setting, but we believe it works best if done at least over the course of several hours and within some kind of community context. Prayerfully consider who you might invite to join you on this journey either before, during, or after the retreat.

Feel no need to race through the material. There is no prize for finishing the exercises before anyone else. The goal is to get a deeper perspective on one's life and relationship with God and this simply cannot be rushed.

Taking retreats like this are part of a healthy life with God, and everyone takes time to refine their "Rule of Life" over the course of several weeks, months, years, or even a lifetime.

So give yourself permission to linger longer on certain sessions. Revisit them more than once because insight usually comes from repeating questions to yourself (and to God) and meditating on them. If you have come to this retreat with others, be sure to leave some discussion time to discuss what you are learning! There is also ample space provided for notes and reflections at the end of each section.

May God enrich your relationship with Him and remember — He is more eager to do this for us than we are to do it for ourselves.

Rule of Life $(n.)$ ————————————————

A STRUCTURE THAT SUPPORTS SPIRITUAL GROWTH AND LIFE

WHAT IS A RULE OF LIFE?

A Rule of Life is an ancient tool used to record what we do in order to maintain a vital interior life with Jesus. Whether it is written down or understood as "personal habits," everyone who pursues God consistently has a Rule of Life, the most basic example being when people say, "I read my Bible and pray daily; also, I go to church every week."

The Rule is modeled after Christ's way of walking with God while in this world. For us, to be spiritual is not some ethereal and merely hopeful thing where we throw up our hands and say, "I hope God does something in my life today!" Instead, to follow Christ's example, we are to be incarnational—embracing what it means to be fully spiritual and fully human. Jesus was God in the flesh. He was perfectly and completely God and therefore spiritual; At the same time He was perfectly, completely human (flesh) and therefore deeply entrenched in the natural way of doing things.

Because of this we understand that for us to have spiritual lives like Jesus, we have to acknowledge and engage our humanity. Great spirituality does not happen automatically or without our cooperation from a human standpoint—for us, the supernatural requires being natural. Great spirituality should not look like escapism from the realities of this world or a deferment of our responsibilities. Merely hoping for God to "show up" is not only wishful thinking but outside the norm demonstrated for us by the incarnation.

Therefore, a Rule is a list of things we **DO** in order to make room for God to act in our lives. Like Elijah who built an altar and put a sacrifice on it, trusting God would send His holy fire upon it, we are to build an altar of habits for God to send fire upon. We are to be the living sacrifices who get on the altar and stay upon it, day after day, and a Rule helps us to do this.

REFLECTION

Have you thought about your spirituality like this before? Is your spirituality incarnational (making use of the body and the spirit) or simply one or the other? Do you have a balance or a preference of one or the other? How might you be enriched by embracing both?

Benefits of a Rule

One primary benefit of keeping a Rule is to have more God in your life and to be more Christlike.

A Rule helps us to order our lives around what is most important and to be aware of our choices and responsibilities. Over time, we will notice our lives gradually changing simply by changing what we do everyday.

This is because the Rule provides an incarnational (natural and supernatural) framework through which the Holy Spirit can inhabit our lives. It helps us to be intentional with our spiritual growth, to know where we are making progress in our spiritual lives, and to become humbly aware of where we need the most help.

For example, how many times have we sought to build a new discipline in our lives, only to try for a little while, get discouraged or absent minded, and then quit? Use of a Rule helps prevent this. It is a tried and proven tool (after all, it is ancient) to help us become disciples of Jesus Christ, growing in holiness. In fact, a Rule can be so effective in one's life that eventually some of the new disciplines that were difficult to implement at first sometimes end up becoming so second nature for the people practicing them that they can no longer imagine life without those healthful practices.

Making
Your Own

A Rule of Life is something solid that forces us to change and conform ourselves to it, and yet at the same time can be tailored to fit every individual. It is both personal and corporate, shaping us into more than we are now, but not removing the unique gifts, interests, and personalities God created us to have.

Therefore, a good Rule is a balanced mix between your personal needs and proven spiritual disciplines that have been used throughout the history of the Church.

As you build your Rule you are going to look for disciplines you need to for your own growth. In the following example, these are called "Practices." Were we playing a sport or learning a musical instrument we would need to practice and maintain our current skills and gifts while learning new skills. The same applies to the spiritual life.

Doing more is usually a recipe for exhaustion and disaster. Focus is the key. To use an archery example, this is more about having precise aim with our lives rather than firing more arrows. Therefore, you will also include things you need to stop doing in order to make room for growth or to stop hindering growth (these are called "Limitations" in the following example).

On the next page is a sample of what a completed Rule looks like. **Just get the overview for now. We will break it down into steps later.**

SAMPLE RULE

LIFE PURPOSE / To live for God's glory, and not my own. *"So whether you eat or drink, or whatever you do, do all to the glory of God."* — 1 Corinthians 10:31

Practices

DAILY

- 15 minutes in Scripture (reading and memorization)
- 15 minutes of prayer

WEEKLY

- A day of rest (sabbath)
- Church attendance
- 30 minutes of devotional reading
- Pray with my spouse about family concerns

MONTHLY

- Fast one meal
- Meet with a friend to discuss things on my heart
- Serve at the food pantry
- Review personal budget and spending

YEARLY

- Give 10% of annual income (tithe)
- Take communion at least 4 times

ONE TIME OR AS NEEDED

- Go on an overnight prayer retreat to discern calling
- Meet with a spiritual director

Limitations

DAILY

- Spirituality before technology (read my Bible or pray before I interact with a screen)
- No technology in bed or late at night

WEEKLY

- Limit on-screen entertainment (computer, TV, other) to 8 hours/week

MONTHLY

- Only make online purchases once a month

YEARLY

- Do not overspend on Christmas presents
- Do not play fantasy football this year

ONE TIME OR AS NEEDED

- Declutter house of excess items
- Cancel Netflix account
- Delete Facebook app from phone

Putting it all Together

Take some time to discern where your heart is right now. Write your reflections on the following pages. Here are a few questions to get you started:

1. What do you already do as a Rule of Life?

2. How might taking the time to craft a Rule of Life benefit you?

3. Do you feel like a personalized Rule of Life is needed for you? Why or why not?

4. Are you intimidated or filled with hope at the prospect of making your own Rule of Life?

5. Regarding the Sample Rule, which practices are you drawn to? Which ones do not apply?

6. What kind of limitations would be most difficult for you?

NOTES

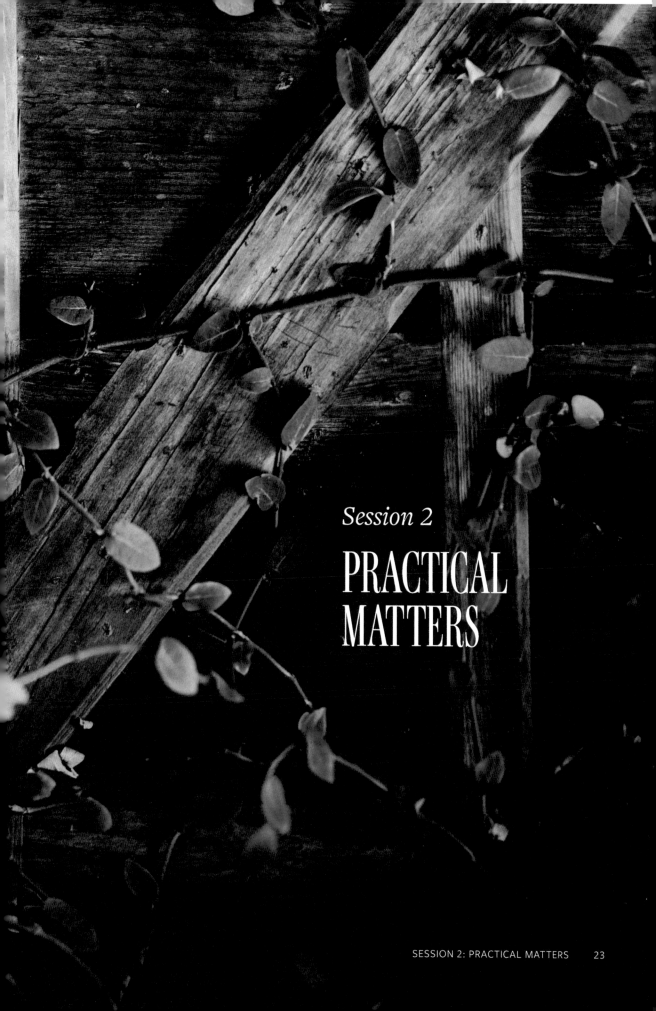

Session 2

PRACTICAL MATTERS

An Assortment of Disciplines

Read through the following list of spiritual disciplines. Take note of which ones appeal to you or even seem to call out as something God would have you grow in. Do not be afraid of a good challenge to help you grow where you are weak, but also beware of places where you might just be striving to perform. You must know yourself—some disciplines just will not be for you, and that's perfectly fine.

This is an extensive list; no one does all of these. There are also plenty of disciplines not found on this list. You may mix, match, and customize each of these to suit your needs. This is just to get you brainstorming about how you might be more intentional and disciplined in your walk with God. The goal is to find practices that help you meet with the Living God.

USING SCRIPTURE

- **Reading Your Bible Devotionally** — This is the classic, tried and true method of getting one's heart and mind focused on God.
- **Developing Biblical Literacy** — This goes hand-in-hand with reading the Bible devotionally, but this is about developing the skill set of reading the Bible. It includes knowing the history, paradigms, background of the languages, etc., that gives one understanding as they read the sacred text.
- **Praying Scripture** — Read through Scripture slowly and meditatively for insight and practical application to your life, and pray it back to God.
- **Praying the Lord's Prayer** — Pray slowly and deliberately through examples from each part of the prayer (for example, "Forgive us our debts" and then naming known sins you have committed).
- **Praying the Psalms** — Do you lack the language of prayer? Pray through the Psalms to shape the way you pray. As you pray them, be mindful of inserting your own situations into the prayers, personalizing each one.
- **Memorizing Scripture** — Fight back against discouraging or negative thoughts by memorizing scripture and bringing it to mind when needed.

PRAYER/MEDITATION

- **The Examen** — At the end of each day, take time to pray and reflect on where you saw God at work. Consider what follow-up actions are needed in response— perhaps confession, forgiving yourself and others, and determining ways you can live differently tomorrow.
- **Silence** — Silence noises and voices around you so you can reflect and hear God's leading (stay away from social media, TV, etc. for a period of time).
- **Journaling** — Write down prayers, insights from Scripture, and God's guidance. Writing things down focuses wandering minds.
- **Sacred Commuting** — Often we are all alone when driving, and this can be a sacred time. Try reserving part of your daily commute for prayer and worship or listening to Scripture instead of working or taking phone calls.

DISCIPLINES OF THE BODY

- **Fasting** — Just as we cry out with our voices or our hearts toward God, so also fasting causes our bodies to cry out to God with every groan of craving and forces us to learn self-control and dependence on God instead of food.
- **Walk and Talk** — You can pray and move! Go on a walk or run to pray, offer thanks, listen to Scripture or sermons, or pray memorized prayers. For centuries, monks did this while tilling soil or gardening.
- **Lying Prostrate or Kneeling Before God in Prayer** — Sometimes just taking a different posture helps us to focus. Most any other discipline can be combined with this discipline of posturing ourselves in humility before God.

PRE-WRITTEN MATERIALS

- **Liturgies** — Pray through pre-written liturgies such as The Daily Office.
- **Devotionals** — Read a devotional or other prayer-provoking book. Do not rush through reading: pause, underline important things, and pray in response as you read to enrich your prayer time.
- **Breath Prayer** — A breath prayer is a one-line prayer from Scripture or a hymn to think and pray on repeatedly throughout the day. Examples of such prayers are, "Lord have mercy on me, a sinner" or "Be near me Lord Jesus, I ask Thee to stay."

COMMUNITY DISCIPLINES

- **Church Attendance** — In a busy society we can easily neglect this essential discipline. How much do we prioritize this? "Do not forsake the assembling of yourselves together" (Hebrews 10:25).
- **Praying with Others** — This is a habit that requires coordination but can be very rewarding for those who struggle to pray by themselves.
- **Confession of Sin** — We should certainly confess our sins to God in private, but our spiritual growth accelerates when we become skilled and regular in confessing sins to one another that we may be healed. Prayerfully consider what trustworthy people or ministers you have in your life with whom you can practice this regularly (1 John 1:9, James 5:16).
- **Fellowship** — This is not just hanging out with friends but intentional conversations about God, spiritual growth, confession of sin, and exchanges of "best practices" for spiritual growth.
- **Taking Communion** — Christ Himself practiced this with His disciples as a way of remembering the Gospel. It is important to find ways to include this in our lives and to ask Christ to give us more of Him and less of us during such times.

SERVICE TO OTHERS

- **Connect Service to Your Devotional Life** — All prayer and Scripture reading must have an outlet and eventual application for others or they grow stale within us. We should see service to others as an essential part of becoming who we are meant to be. It starts with asking God, "Where am I called to serve others?" In all these things be careful to do so with the heart of giving service and glory to God.
- **In Your Church** — Every church has needs. Do your gifts meet these needs?
- **Outside of Your Church** — A great way to help people come to know Christ is to serve with them in your community. Approaching things in a godly way and with godly motivations is a witness for Christ.
- **In Your Workplace** — Sometimes our best ministry opportunities are those God gives us through our workplace. We should be on the lookout for ways to love and serve others around us at work.
- **In Your Heart to Do** — Nehemiah had a vision for doing something that no one else was acting on. We should ask ourselves about our hopes and dreams for our

community and see if there is something God is calling us to act on (Nehemiah 2:12).

- **Financial Giving** — Are you called to go above and beyond in your giving? At the very least we should be intentional about our financial contributions to our churches and community. Consider rallying others to similar causes. We see Paul doing this all the time in Scripture, and we are to follow him as he followed Christ. What are you passionate about and can you invite others to help build God's Kingdom in a similar way?

REFLECTION

Now, go back through and circle or underline the ones you feel drawn to explore.

Of all the disciplines, people usually need the most help getting their prayer life going because it is one of the most challenging and least often talked about disciplines in Church life. To that end, the remainder of this session will be spent on suggestions for setting up one's personal prayer times with God.

Sacred Space and Time Considerations

—

You need a good place to pray regularly. This might be the library, a local coffee shop, or a place outside. For most people, it will be somewhere in their home. Having a sacred space in one's home is an ancient Christian practice. Believers used to gather in private residences—there were no church buildings as we know them now for the first few centuries of the faith. Archaeologists have discovered altars built in Christian homes where believers would gather on the Lord's Day to worship and celebrate communion. Were you and I living at this time, it would not be uncommon for us to say our prayers at those same altar places throughout the week. This was the context in which much of the New Testament was written. When the Apostle Paul addressed believers, he was talking to Christians who would have had a sacred space set up in their homes.

When Christianity became legalized and no longer had to stay hidden in homes, glorious formal church buildings were constructed almost overnight. This did not, however, mean that Christians ceased having dedicated spaces in their houses for the worship of God. Instead, believers kept their altars and went to their separate church buildings. This practice has continued to the present day with many Catholic and Orthodox believers maintaining a dedicated sacred space in their homes as an important practical piece of personal piety. These spaces are always set up intentionally—they often occupy a nook or corner of the house and come complete with sacred art and crosses on the wall, small tables set up with candles, colored cloth, prayer books, and sometimes one even finds kneelers or comfy rugs to lie prostrate on.

This kind of decor may not suit the fancy of everyone reading this, but we should recognize that sacred spaces in the homes of believers was a practice of the same early Church that turned the world upside down. We would do well to emulate this practice. Remember, whatever we want to happen supernaturally in our lives works best if we have a natural counterpart. The same applies with a sacred space to pray.

For us, this may mean clearing out a closet and storing stuff elsewhere so we can have a tiny private room to pray in. It may mean putting a desk or kneeler in some place off the most beaten paths of our homes. Wherever we set it up, it should be sacred and have the accoutrements required for prayer. Make a list of prayer topics/requests and post it to a bulletin board—put up whatever physical prompts you find helpful for your prayer life. Regardless, the space should say one thing to you: Christ is the welcomed and precious Guest of your home, and this is the place where you will meet Him.

If you cannot set up a space or if that idea just seems alien to you, then find a favorite place where you can pray—one that is comfy but not so comfy you fall asleep. It may be a desk or a favorite couch with a great end table to place your coffee on.

One critical thing: the space should be undisturbed—at least for the time you are going to use it—and it should be free from distractions (TV, computer, etc.). If you are going to answer your phone, then do not bring it with you. If your spaces happens to be your desk and some work is on it, or it is in a room with some unfinished house project that will nag you in the back of your mind the whole time you are praying then you probably do not have the right location.

In general, you want to make sure you do not have to think about where you are going to pray when the time comes. It should be a known, previously thought through decision that has already been made. Praying in a distracted or frequently disturbed place can discourage us from starting or maintaining a steady practice of prayer.

REFLECTION

Where should I pray? What do I need to do to feel comfortable and motivated in that place? Am I sure the place I am thinking of works? What might get in the way of that location? Is there another place that works better?

The Right Stuff

During my years of youth ministry I made sure my kids had their "PBJs" ready when we went on retreats. That is "P" for pencil or pen, "B" for Bible, and "J" for journals to write in. During our sessions together, whether it was listening to a speaker or praying and worshipping together, I wanted them ready to interact with however God might speak to them. That might mean writing a thought down or looking something up in Scripture. Having their PBJs with them and being prepared was helpful in their spiritual walk.

This principle applies to a lot of things, and our interactions with God are no different. Imagine if church was interrupted because the pastor or worship team were unprepared. The church service may still go well, but you may have a harder time connecting with God because of the disjointed nature of their unprepared service. Our focus can be broken away from supernatural things just as it can natural things. Therefore, when you enter prayer times, know what you generally are going to need when you are in the right place for praying.

Here is a list of what most people make good use of during their prayer times:

Notebook or Scratch Paper for Distractions

This is one of the most often used items. The instant you stop to pray your mind will be distracted with various thoughts. This happens a lot, especially in the first few months of learning to pray and quiet our souls. When it does happen, just write down the distractions that come to mind knowing you can surrender these ideas to the piece of paper because you will come back to them later.

Pen or Pencil

Use it to write down the distractions or great ideas that come to you in prayer or to underline things in your Bible or the devotional book you are reading. Future Bible studies can be greatly enriched by notes taken in your Bible during your prayer times, so do not be squeamish about adding a little of your own ink to the pages.

Bible

Having the Bible nearby lets you reference it easily. A tablet or phone is not usually a good idea because it makes us much more vulnerable to distractions instead of praying.

Background Music

So much of the Psalms (which are easily among the greatest prayers ever composed) were to be spoken or sung to music. In 2 Kings 3:15, when Elisha was seeking the Lord for an answer, he specifically requested a harpist to come and play. As soon as the harpist did, God's power came to rest on the prophet, and while I cannot say the exact same thing will happen to any of us if we pray with music in the background, I believe the principle still applies: music is an aid to prayer.

When selecting music, try to make it something that will help you to pray and not distract you. It may be worship music you sing along with, instrumental selections without words, or Gregorian Chant or Russian Orthodox Church music that lifts your heart to God.

Liturgies

There is absolutely nothing wrong with praying pre-written prayers. Christians have been doing this for centuries and praying the same prayers over and over helps shape our souls. There are many great resources for this—liturgies, The Daily Office, the *Book of Common Prayer*, etc. Christian devotionals by many authors as well as Scripture compilations exist for this purpose. Some people even keep an old hymnal and pray through the rich words instead of singing them. Search these out to find one that works for you, and pray as God leads!

Praying repetitiously can be found throughout the book of Psalms (which are written down as a prayer book for us to use over and over again); Psalm 136 is probably the preeminent example for refrains in prayer. Jesus Himself said the exact same words three times in the Garden of Gethsemane (Matthew 26:44, Mark 14:39). If the sinless Christ can pray like this, then of course we can as well. This is helpful for creating well-worn paths in our minds and hearts to follow God more closely in particular areas.

Other aids for prayer are having a set order in which you are going to pray each time. For example, A.C.T.S.—where you offer prayers of **A**doration, **C**onfession, **T**hanksgiving, and **S**upplication. You could also use prayer beads or ropes to help order your prayers. (This is NOT just a Catholic thing. It is an ancient Christian practice as well and used by the Orthodox, Catholics, and varieties of Protestants today.)

REFLECTION

Do I have the right stuff to pray that suits my own personal style? Are there any liturgies I could make use of?

Sacred Time

THE RIGHT TIME

—

Everyone is different. There will be people who love praying first thing in the morning, others will make it the last thing they do before sleep, and still there are a few people who find the lunch hour to be their best time to pray consistently. There will even be some who mix up those times on a regular basis just to keep it interesting. Do not judge yourself or others for having different habits—just find what works best for you, and help others to do the same.

A few pointers: you want to be alert, so don't choose a time you are going to fall asleep or fall back to sleep. Pay attention to your personal needs and pray accordingly. For example, if your job is stressful and you find yourself needing to prepare your heart, pray in the morning before going to work! If you need to reset your mind during the day, pray at your lunch break. If your days are packed, pick a time in the evening to pray (it is better than watching Hulu).

Lots of people benefit from multiple times of prayer during the day. For example, when you first wake up, before you reach for your cell phone or your feet hit the floor, a basic prayer is useful to set one's heart and mind toward Jesus. Likewise, some prayer for hope and trust in God for the following day is great to pray before going to sleep. These prayers do not have to be long, but they augment whatever you set aside as your main time of prayer.

THE RIGHT AMOUNT OF TIME

—

For setting the right amount of time, you have to answer two questions:

1. Why are you praying?
2. What works best to accomplish your reason for prayer?

If you are praying to refocus yourself during your day, you may just need 5 minutes at lunchtime. If you are interceding for a specific situation, set a timer or alarm to remind you to pray.

If, however, your prayer is meant for more of a personal discipleship time where you sit at the feet of Jesus to enjoy His presence and learn from Him, you probably need a little longer. If that is the case, you probably do not want to set aside less than 15 minutes. Why 15 minutes? For whatever reason that seems to be the minimal amount needed for people to calm down and switch gears so they get into a sweet spot of focusing on Jesus.

There may come a time when you need to set aside extra time to pray. It may be because there is a big question or decision you are processing before the Lord, and you know you need to go to Him.

Perhaps you will find yourself especially hungry for time in God's presence. If this happens to you, please do not ignore those moments of divine calling—respond to them. You may want to go on a personal retreat or at least set aside a whole block of time (3 hours or more) to seek the Lord. Prayer begets prayer in our lives. The more we do it, the more we enjoy it and want it because we find it so life-giving.

SET A GOOD RHYTHM

—

Finally, it is wise to consider how often you will want or need to seek God. In the Gospel accounts we see Jesus consistently talking to His Father, but He does not go away to pray every day.

The way I like to talk about this is to compare hummingbirds with anacondas. The hummingbird burns up its energy quickly and darts around from flower to flower eating multiple meals every day according to its needs. The anaconda does not do this. It takes a long time to swallow just one huge meal and then takes weeks to digest it. People can work the same way in their spiritual lives. There will be some who need to pray intentionally every day multiple times per day, and still others will latch on to just one thing and pray through it over and over for weeks. Both are acceptable to God, and both yield fruit in a believer's life. One way is not more righteous than the other, so learn who you are and be who you are. Don't try to be something you are not meant to be.

Regardless of what you discover works for you, the key is to remain consistent with it. Oswald Chambers, whose brilliant mind and reflections have changed the lives of millions in his bestselling devotional, *My Utmost for His Highest*, said, "A quarter of an hour a day on any subject will make you the master of that subject. Consistency is the key." So while you do not have to overdo it, you still have to do it!

START SMALL, WORK YOUR WAY UP

—

Give Yourself Time for Improvement. One thing to be wary of is trying to do too much. It is better to start small and have great success (as well as encouragement) than to attempt too much, resulting in failure and disappointment. Try to be realistic in assessing what you can do to begin. Rome was not built in a day, and neither are the habits of our hearts. Give yourself time to be rooted and grounded in Christ through prayer.

REFLECTION

All these time factors considered, what works best for you? Do you need a long or short period of time? What time of day works best, and how often? Is there anything going on in your prayer life that needs an extended time of prayer?

NOTES

Session 3

SEARCHING QUESTIONS

Hopefully by now you are starting to get an idea of what you need to create a Rule of Life. The following questions are designed to help you become more intentional about the habits you wish to keep and those you wish to break. This can be done on your own, but it is more useful to discern these rhythms for life with the help of experienced believers coming alongside you. Do not feel it is absolutely necessary to answer each question, and know that some questions will be answered more thoroughly than others. Some of the questions overlap one another in theme. Sometimes we get to the heart of the matter by being asked the same question in different ways. Go with what is most helpful for you. Based on what you have done thus far, some of this might come easy for you.

Searching Questions

1. Start with your life's purpose. Do you know what this is? From this, your Rule should be crafted to reflect who you are and where God is calling you to go. If you already have spiritual disciplines in place, what life purpose do they reflect? (See the example located by the title in the Sample Rule in Session 1.)

2. What are you lacking in your spiritual life? Where are you needing to be formed (not just informed) in the faith? Where do you sense the Spirit calling you to reform your habits?

3*a.* Where are you noticing certain repeated sin patterns or unbelief in your life? In what situations are you most tempted? What are those sins?

_____

_____

_____

_____

_____

_____

_____

_____

_____

_____

_____

_____

3*b.* In response to 3*a*, what specific steps do you need to take (people to talk to, books to read, Scriptures to pray, habits to change)?

_____

_____

_____

_____

_____

_____

_____

_____

_____

_____

_____

_____

3c. What practices can you put in your Rule to consistenly walk out those specific steps listed in *3b*?

_____

_____

_____

_____

_____

_____

_____

_____

_____

_____

_____

_____

3d. Based on your previous answers, what Scriptures best speak into your situation? If helpful, make a list and use these to pray through often.

_____

_____

_____

_____

_____

_____

_____

_____

_____

_____

_____

_____

4. Some disciplines we consistently practice on our own, but for others we need community. Which disciplines can you faithfully practice on your own? Which need community?

_____

_____

_____

_____

_____

_____

_____

_____

_____

_____

_____

5. Say you were your own "coach" of your personal walk with Christ. Looking at your life, what specific actions/habits/practices would you recommend as needed for your spiritual development?

_____

_____

_____

_____

_____

_____

_____

_____

_____

_____

_____

6. What routine do you need to put in place in order to practice these disciplines? Where will you find time for them, and what might you need to give up?

7. Do you need further training or information on any of these practices?

_____

_____

_____

_____

_____

_____

_____

_____

_____

_____

8. From Matthew 13:22: *"As for what was sown among thorns, this is the one who hears the word, but the cares of the world and the deceitfulness of riches choke the word, and it proves unfruitful."* Jesus warns that the cares (tasks and things we need to manage) and deceitfulness of riches (too much of good things) can render the word unfruitful. That being said, take some time to ask God about what "thorns" choke out the seed of life in you. What do you need to avoid or remove from your life?

_____

_____

_____

_____

_____

_____

_____

CRAFTING YOUR RULE

Now is the time to craft your own Rule of Life.

What follows is a basic framework for writing your own Rule of Life—it's just a suggestion—there is no rule for a Rule. If you want to be more creative, feel free to do so. Some people include an introductory page or two to explain why they have written their rule the way they have or to give more of the heart behind the practical side of things. Others are bare-bones minimalists. Whatever helps you love Jesus more, do that.

Framework
for a Rule

LIFE PURPOSE / *Scripture and Summary Statement*

EXAMPLE PRACTICES

Daily or Weekly

- Scripture (reading, memorization, study, etc.)
- Prayer (journal, liturgy, worship, prayer walking, etc.)
- Devotional reading

Weekly

- A day of rest (sabbath)
- Church attendance
- Community (small group, Bible study, etc.)
- Serve others in some capacity

Monthly

- Fasting
- Communion
- Confession of sin
- Day of prayer
- Meet with a spiritual director or mentor
- Invest in a younger person's life
- Look back through your Rule of Life, revise if necessary

Yearly

- Tithing, generous giving
- Annual overnight retreat (with friends or alone)
- Seasonal observations (Lent, Advent, church-wide fast, etc.)

One-Time or as the Need Arises
- Baptism
- Committ to or join your local church

EXAMPLE LIMITATIONS

Daily
- Spirituality before technology (read my Bible or pray before I interact with a screen)
- No technology in bed or late at night

Weekly
- Of the body (consider sleep, food, exercise)
- Limit on-screen entertainment

The following pages are provided to help you craft your Rule.

Crafting Your Rule

Use this space to brainstorm —

Crafting Your Rule

Use this space to brainstorm —

YOUR RULE

Practices

DAILY

WEEKLY

MONTHLY

YEARLY

ONE TIME OR AS NEEDED

Limitations

DAILY

WEEKLY

MONTHLY

YEARLY

ONE TIME OR AS NEEDED

AFTER THE RETREAT

KEEP IT ON HAND

—

Print out your Rule and put it in a place where you are going to see it somewhat regularly. Be sure to review it from time to time in order to not forget the things you set out to do. This is key to keeping your Rule.

COMMUNITY

—

Once we have a Rule, it provides an easy framework for accountability and for the discipleship of others (Would you do this with me? Can we do this together?).

A Rule is best practiced in community. It is much harder to keep on your own.

FOR YOURSELF

—

As you go back to everyday life with your Rule, be mindful that it will be actual as well as aspirational. This is normal. You should have a Rule you are attempting to grow into, but if you find after six months you have set impossibly high expectations for yourself and are making incredibly little progress, you may want to readjust it again until you have grown in discipline. If you have composed this Rule on your own, consider sharing it with others.

RULES FOR FAMILIES

—

You can create a Rule for your entire family.
Go through this guide with your spouse
and kids (if they are old enough) to set
up the kind of *culture* you are aiming for
in your family. Again, this is best done in
community. If you have a small group with
multiple families involved, doing the exercise together is fruitful.

GIVE IT AWAY TO OTHERS

—

A Rule of Faith is also a ready-made discipleship tool. It can easily be given away and shared and can be adapted to any kind of church community. Prayerfully consider asking a friend to do this with you and especially a younger person as well as an older person. We always need to be mentored, and we always need to be giving away what we learn. Both are enriching and important for a sustained and healthy walk with Christ.

Also consider it an evangelistic tool. There are several examples in the history of the Church where societies changed not because of evangelical experiences but because of faithful discipleship. Perhaps most famously, Kievan Russia converted instantly in 988 AD on the order of the Prince; however, the subsequent discipleship of their society into the truth of Christ and the means of following Him is what set them apart. They were so transformed that they in turn became one of the most evangelistic societies in history. That said, do not limit sharing your Rule to only believers. One of the best proofs for Christianity has been the *wisdom of lifestyle* that accompanies the faith, and many have been won to Christ because of it. You may find people of goodwill and an open mind to practice some of these things with you for their own well-being. Do not turn this down as a possible open door from Christ to move their hearts toward Him!

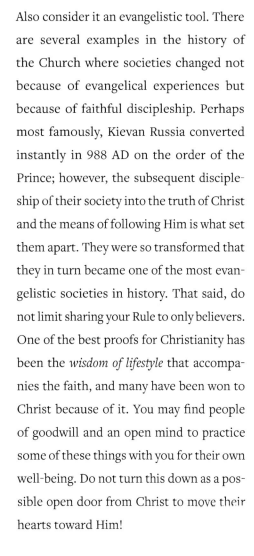

REFLECTION

On the following pages, take a moment to write down some names of people you can follow up with to ask about going on this journey with you.

FINAL THOUGHTS

—

Now is the time to share your Rule with others. Share your reasoning behind the practices you are seeking to keep and what you hope to get out of them.

It would also be helpful to set up regular follow-up times with a friend to discuss your new Rule, refine it, and encourage one another.

Also, do not get discouraged if you fail at keeping your Rule. If you do not come from a faith tradition where this is practiced, or you are not used to being so intentional in this area, a Rule of Life can initially be quite difficult to get off the ground. A lot of people write it out, forget about it, see it again in a few months, and then remember what they set out to do. The key is being persistent. God will honor your faithfulness!

NOTES

WAYS TO STAY INVOLVED

LEARN MORE

To find more resources and opportunities to grow in prayer, visit *ChattHOP.org*.

SPREAD THE WEALTH

We are eager to share this retreat guide with people in our city and beyond. If you need assistance in hosting a retreat using our resources, please do not hesitate to contact us at *admin@ChattHOP.org*.

FOLLOW US

Facebook — Chattanooga House of Prayer

Instagram — @chattanoogahouseofprayer

—

Subscribe to our emails by visiting *ChattHOP.org/newsletter*.

For Retreat Facilitators

A NOTE TO THOSE LEADING A RETREAT

—

Let the Holy Spirit be the primary presenter for the retreat. Resist the urge to speak too much.

As far as retreat locations are concerned, you will want to find a place where noise and distractions are limited. It is helpful to have space to gather as a group and space where participants can pray privately.

Each retreat is broken up into times of instruction and times of reflection. Ideally, you know the people you are facilitating well enough to discern how much time is needed for each of these sections. Since this is something that must be intuited by you rather than given in a formula, there have been no precise amounts of time given. We have included several sample retreat schedules to help you construct your own when making a retreat. Also feel free to reach out to us if you have questions (email ***admin@ ChattHOP.org***).

Sample Retreat Schedules

HALF DAY RETREAT

For this shortened retreat, the facilitator will need to give brief overviews of the material and let people read through it more thoroughly later.

8:00 am	Breakfast and Fellowship
8:15	Retreat Introduction
8:20	Session 1: What is a Rule of Life?
8:50	Session 2: Practical Matters
9:30	Session 3: Searching Questions
10:15	Break
10:25	Session 4: Crafting Your Rule
11:10	Discussion and Group Workshop
11:40	Session 5: After the Retreat
12:00 pm	Prayer of Blessing and Dismiss

DAY RETREAT

9:00 am	Welcome and Retreat Introduction
9:15	Session 1: What is a Rule of Life?
10:00	Discussion and Prayer
10:30	Break
10:45	Session 2: Practical Matters
11:45	Discussion and Prayer
12:00	Lunch, Continued Discussion, Fellowship
1:00	Session 3: Searching Questions
2:00	Discussion and Prayer
2:30	Session 4: Crafting Your Rule

3:30	Discussion and Group Workshop
4:00	Session 5: After the Retreat
4:30	Discussion and Prayer
5:00 pm	Prayer of Blessing and Dismiss

OVERNIGHT RETREAT

Evening

7:00 pm	Welcome and Retreat Introduction
7:30	Session 1: What is a Rule of Life?
8:15	Discussion and Group Prayer
9:00	Free Time

Day 2

8:00 am	Breakfast
8:45	Session 2: Practical Matters
9:45	Discussion and Group Prayer
10:15	Break
10:30	Session 3: Searching Questions
12:00	Discussion and Group Prayer
12:30	Lunch, Continued Discussion, Fellowship
1:30	Session 4: Crafting Your Rule
2:30	Discussion and Group Workshop
3:30	Session 5: After the Retreat
4:00	Discussion and Group Prayer
5:00 pm	Prayer of Blessing and Dismiss

WEEKEND RETREAT

Friday Night

7:00 pm	Welcome and Retreat Introduction
7:30	Session 1: What is a Rule of Life?
8:15	Discussion and Group Prayer
9:00	Free Time

Saturday

8:00 am	Breakfast
8:45	Worship
9:00	Session 2: Practical Matters
10:00	Discussion
10:30	Break
10:45	Session 3: Searching Questions
12:00	Discussion
12:30	Lunch, Continued Discussion, Fellowship
1:30	Group Prayer of Blessing One Another
2:00	Session 4: Crafting Your Rule
3:30	Discussion and Group Workshop
4:30	Free Time
6:30	Dinner
7:30	Worship and Prayer
9:00 pm	Free Time

Sunday

8:00 am	Breakfast
9:00	Worship and Preaching
10:30	Session 5: After the Retreat
11:00	Group Prayer and Discussion
11:30	Prayer of Blessing and Dismiss

Photo Credits

Made in the USA
Columbia, SC
24 March 2022

58101919R10042